Author's GUIDE to Children's Book Promotion

Susan Salzman Raab

Published by

Raab Associates Inc.

345 Millwood Road
Chappaqua, NY 10514
www.raabassociates.com

April 2007
Tenth Edition
ISBN 09621211-7-7

Foreword

I feel very fortunate to have spent more than twenty years in the children's book business. In that time, many people have generously shared their knowledge about the business. This book was written to relay what I've learned to authors and illustrators in the hope that it will provide ideas and contacts that contribute to the success of their books.

First published in 1988, this book has been expanded to cover more areas of marketing, publicity, promotion, and the Internet. Many additions came in response to questions authors and illustrators have asked since the first edition was published.

Special thanks for this edition go to Joan Honig, Jeanette Larson and Joyce Stein.

Susan Salzman Raab

TABLE OF CONTENTS

INTRODUCTION

Book promotion is the author's job. Whether you are a top name at a major publishing house or a new author, your book is more important to you than to anyone else. Consequently, you will devote the most time and energy to promoting your product. And, as the author of a children's book, your role is even more important.

In the past, the success of a children's book hinged on sales to schools and libraries. Children's books were not big business for most bookstores or publishing houses. Today that has changed. The sale of children's and young adult books has become a major part of the book industry..

New publishers and self-published authors enter the market regularly. In recent years, the independent children's-only bookstores have been pressed to compete with book chains, superstores, mass merchandisers and now Internet booksellers, making it more difficult for individual titles to compete with series books for shelf space.

However, the larger outlets have made volume buying of children's titles more prevalent. Sales to schools have also increased as more paperbacks are used in the classroom. The impact of the Internet is still evolving and niche marketing and sales opportunities are growing rapidly.

As important as juvenile books are, however, authors should realize that of the 149,859 trade books published in 2005, only 15,982 were children's and young adult titles — less than 11 percent. So it is easy to understand why even the most committed publishers of children's books have limited resources to devote to each title. In addition, publishers' costs increase when they hold onto stock that isn't selling so most books have only a short time to prove themselves.

That is why your efforts will be important. And they will probably be appreciated as long as you work in cooperation with your editor and the marketing staff.

This guide is designed to help you make the most of opportunities to sell and promote your book. It includes ideas for marketing, promoting, and publicizing your book. There are also sample formats for promotional materials and a directory of key organizations, contacts, and source materials.

Every author's book is unique and you will have to be creative to determine how these ideas apply to your book. Many will apply whether your book is self-published or published by a major publishing house.

Be sure to refer to the directory for information on industry awards, conventions, publications, and groups that may be of interest. The directory also lists addresses, telephone numbers, and web site URL's for publications and organizations mentioned in other parts of this book.

You might also want to visit the "To Market" section of the Raab Associates, Inc. website at *www.raabassociates.com* for additional information.

CHAPTER 1

Helping Your Publisher

According to Robert J. R. Follett, author of *The Financial Side of Book Publishing* (Ad-Lib Publications), approximately 5 percent of a book's cover price is allocated for promotion and publicity. Most of that money goes toward catalog listings and space advertising. The remainder is allotted to other types of promotion and publicity, including trade advertising, conventions and exhibits, and public relations.

It is important for an author to know that the publisher's commitment to promoting new titles will increase as the company publishes more of the author's books. But whether you are a first time author or an established house author, there are ways that you can work with the publisher to help promote your book.

Opinions on how much an author should do vary. Many publishers encourage authors to do publicity in their local communities and to get on the lecture circuit to schools and libraries. Some will guide and support authors who want to extend the house's publicity and marketing efforts. Others may try to discourage authors from participating because they are afraid an author will become too demanding or will hinder the publisher's own efforts.

However, it is very unlikely that any publisher would do less for your book because you are promoting it. The more the book gets promoted, the more everyone will benefit.

Whatever your level of activity, be sure to discuss your promotion or publicity plans, especially those that will involve the publisher, in advance with your editor or the marketing staff. You don't want to duplicate or conflict with their efforts, and they don't need any surprises. Keep them informed of your progress and report on your results. This may give them ideas for marketing possibilities for your future books.

Author Biography and Photograph

The editorial, promotion, and publicity departments will need copies of a current biography and a recent portrait photograph prior to publication of your book. Submit the biography and photograph to your editor with the manuscript. They can be used on the book jacket when the book is published or on the publisher's web site. Plan to submit copies to the promotion and publicity departments eight to ten months in advance of your book's publication date for use in catalogs and other promotional and publicity materials. Consider updating your biography and photograph with each new book.

You may use an existing photograph of yourself, have a photographer friend take a new photograph, or hire a professional. Your portrait photograph should be color; the preferred size is 5 x 7 inches. Send an electronic file formatted as a .jpeg, in addition to a printed copy.

When writing your biographical sketch, include pertinent educational and work background as well as titles and publishers of other books published. A few personal details about your current activities and work in progress may also be of interest to readers.

The information you provide will probably be used to create copy for the book jacket and the publisher's catalogue and included in publicity materials. Your biographical sketch may also be used to develop a brochure for distribution at conventions and to schools, or for a profile on the publisher's web site.

Each publishing house has its own policy for deciding how

many authors each season get special attention and which books are chosen. These are not done for every author the house publishes; the decision is likely to be made based on how many of that author's books are on the publisher's list and how well the author's books sell. Sometimes a brochure, or web mention, will be done to coincide with a special press kit or publicity campaign the publisher is doing for a particular book.

If your publisher does author brochures, or web pages, obtain samples for other authors and write your own copy to fit the style. Submit the copy with a current photograph that you would like used to your editor and publicist and ask them to consider printing a brochure or including a web mention for you. Since you've done the bulk of the work, they are more likely to agree, provided there are funds available in the promotion budget.

Author Appearances

Publishers often receive requests for authors to appear at schools, libraries, conferences, and other events. Some event coordinators want a specific author and will pay a sizable honorarium fee plus travel expenses to get that person. Many others have limited budgets and are happy to find a local author who will charge less for participating in the event.

The lower your honorarium and the more available you are for author appearances, the easier it will be for your publisher to place you at events. New authors should consider setting their rates lower than average ($500 - $1000) until they get established on the lecture circuit. Ask your publisher for advice on setting your honorarium rate. Generally, schools and libraries are accustomed to paying an honorarium; bookstores normally do not expect to pay. Once established, you may want to consider hiring a school booking agency to help with negotiations and arrangements.

Keep your publisher informed of any travel plans that could include time for one or more appearances. There are almost sure to be bookstores, schools, and libraries in the area that would like to host a visit. Sometimes the publisher's marketing department will know of a specific school in that area that is interested in arranging an author visit, but has limited money for travel. Many children's bookstores have well-developed relationships with one or more local schools and will be interested in coordinating a school visit, with or without an appearance, at the bookstore.

You can benefit by having your trip become a business trip for tax purposes and by receiving an honorarium. The school will get a break on the travel. Your book will get added visibility. And, with sufficient notice, it may be possible to obtain local media interviews as well.

If your publisher has promotional posters, bookmarks, brochures, teacher's guides, or other materials that include your book, keep a supply on hand to bring with you to bookstores, schools, libraries, and conventions that you plan to attend. Ask the publisher to send additional quantities when it is appropriate, but try to anticipate your needs so that you will not have to make frequent requests for supplies. Some of these materials can also be used as enclosures in your replies to letters from young readers.

Consider creating an audio or video tape for the publisher, answering common questions about you and your writing. The publisher may be able to sell or loan copies of the tape to teachers or others who cannot arrange a personal visit or interview. This is particularly useful for an established author who has limited time for personal appearances.

Keep in mind that the cost for professional production and editing of a video is quite high and would normally be budgeted only for well-established authors. At an average cost of around $1,000 per minute, a video may not necessarily be the best use of funds. However, with the help of a talented amateur you may be able to develop a good video or audiotape, and the cost to duplicate tapes is modest. A video is also helpful if there's interest in booking you as a guest on TV.

Publisher's Newsletters

Some publishers produce and distribute newsletters on their children's books, or feature news about children's books in other house publications. Publisher generated emails are becoming an increasingly popular format for book news. Copies may go to key buyers, wholesalers, booksellers, educators, librarians, and the media. Newsletters are also used to keep people within the company abreast of news about books and authors.

These publications can include information on forthcoming books, author profiles, author appearances, and award announcements. Find out whether your publisher has this kind of publication. If so, keep the newsletter editor apprised of your appearances and activities.

Request back issues of the newsletter to better understand what kinds of material you might contribute. Sometimes newsletters are archived on the publisher's web site. Offer to write an article on a topic in which you have expertise if that seems appropriate.

Suggesting Publicity Angles and Outlets

The publisher will appreciate any suggestions that can contribute to book sales as long as you present your ideas in a reasonable way. Prepare ideas in advance and begin your discussion when you sign the contract; then submit them in writing to your publisher as soon after that as possible to allow for them to decide if and how your requests will factor into their promotion plans.

Subsequent suggestions should also be submitted in writing. Your publisher will likely provide direction for contacts within the organization once your book has been published. You may continue to communicate primarily with your editor, or you may be assigned a contact person in the publicity department. In any case, the children's book publicist typically does many different jobs, has responsibility for many authors, and is given very little staff to help get the work done. Your relationship will be most productive if you are careful to limit your telephone calls to issues that require an immediate response and provide concrete suggestions for publicity that can be easily executed. Give plenty of advance notice of special promotion and publicity opportunities that are time-sensitive and require action by the publicist.

As its author, you know more about your book than anyone else. Your publisher may ask you to complete a standard author questionnaire. Be sure to include what you consider to be unique points of interest about your book. Discuss your reasons for writing the book. Explain why you think this book is newsworthy or different from other books on the topic.

Suggest special-interest groups that might be interested in purchasing quantities of the book. For example, a book dealing with AIDS might qualify for inclusion on a recommended reading list published by the Center for Disease Control. Or you may belong to one or more organizations whose members are potential buyers. If the organization's web site has a section that includes news about members, the publication of your new book is almost certain to be worthy of inclusion.

List any experiences you have in giving speeches, conducting seminars and workshops, doing press and broadcast interviews, and writing press or promotional material.

Provide your publisher with the names of personal contacts you have who may be able to help sell or publicize your book. There's no reason to be shy about sending a review copy to a neighbor who writes for the local bureau of the Associated Press. Even if she doesn't cover issues related to your book, she may recommend the book to someone who does. Many of your friends and relatives are also likely to be enthusiastic buyers of your book, and your publisher may be interested in sending an announcement to those individuals. Offer to provide a set of names on labels. You might also want to supply a list of e-mail addresses.

CHAPTER II

Getting Your Book Distributed: Wholesalers, Retailers, Direct Marketing, Special Sales

The following sections on wholesalers, getting national distribution and retail sales are primarily geared to authors whose books are self-published. Publishers will generally have sales and subsidiary rights departments that will handle sales of your book. Some authors do supplement the publisher's efforts by getting involved with niche marketing and special sales. Be sure to check with your publishing house before pursuing sales opportunities on your own.

Wholesalers

About half of the independent (non-chain) bookstores in the country buy only through national wholesalers such as Ingram and Baker & Taylor, or through regional wholesalers such as Partners and Bookazine. Contact The American Wholesale Booksellers Association for a list of wholesalers.

If you have self-published, it can be quite difficult to convince key wholesalers to carry your book.These companies work primarily with the major publishers and generally require evidence that there is a strong demand in the marketplace before they will consider stocking a book. It will be up to you to create that demand.

You can do this through publicity, which may generate consumer interest and requests from booksellers, who will then special order the book from wholesalers. Wholesalers track such requests and will take notice of demand even for a book they do not have in stock. Make sure to let the wholesalers know what reviewers have said about the book.

Or you can start by convincing stores that are most likely to give your book some attention, like children's-only stores, to help you establish a track record of sales.

Retailers

Local Retailers

Your best bet, when you are first beginning to sell your book, is to start locally. If you can prove that your book can sell there, you can gradually extend your sales regionally and then nationally.

Local booksellers are likely to be interested in carrying your book, especially if you are willing to help them sell it, for example, by participating in a Saturday morning story hour. You may want to offer your book on consignment, so that the bookseller takes no risk.

Toy stores and gift shops often carry children's books. Approach store managers to find out if they will consider carrying your book in their store.

Once you have approached local bookstores and other local outlets, contact the juvenile book buyers at local book chains to find out whether they would consider carrying your book. Be sure to let them know if the book has any local interest beyond local authorship.

Book Fairs

Get involved with book fairs that are being held at local schools, libraries, and community centers. You may be able to set up your own table to sell books if you are willing to donate a portion of the proceeds to the hosting organization, or you may offer to come and autograph books that have been purchased by the book fair organizer.

Local book fairs are often managed by a local independent bookseller or by a school or other sponsoring organization. However, many are supplied by national book fair companies like Scholastic Book Clubs, and by specialized wholesalers and catalogers. Your book would need a very strong sales record to be considered for inclusion in their pre-selected book fair assortments.

Getting National Retail Distribution

Once you decide to sell outside your geographic area, you may want to consider hiring independent sales representatives who sell regionally or nationally. Check *Literary Market Place* for a listing of book representatives or rep groups, who generally cover one of the 8-10 traditional geographic territories in the country. Talk to other publishers for recommendations. You will have to work hard to convince the best independent reps to carry your book. They will need to feel confident that your book can earn its place in their "bag" before they make a commitment of time and energy to selling it. Be prepared to negotiate commission rates (generally 10-12%) and such issues as whether orders that booksellers place through national wholesalers will be commissionable.

If you enjoy sales, and have the time, don't be afraid to act as your own representative. Pick up the phone and call children's bookstores outside your immediate area. Prepare a simple script about yourself and your book and why the bookseller should try it. Sending a bookseller a free reader copy is likely to generate an order for multiple copies. Be sure to enclose a simple letter or flyer that includes all necessary ordering information. For a list of several hundred bookstores with a strong emphasis on juvenile books, contact the Association of Booksellers for Children.

To gain national distribution, send copies of your book to children's book buyers at chain bookstores, such as Barnes & Noble or Borders.

Amazon.com and *BarnesandNoble.com* are the leading Internet retailers, and they have a large section of children's books. If you would prefer to find local, independent stores, you can check for locations at *booksense.com*, a referral service of the American Booksellers Association

Tell the buyers why you think they might be interested in carrying your book. Include information on how the book has sold in other outlets, and which distributors stock the book. Enclose copies of positive reviews the book has received, and tell them where you live in case they are interested in carrying the book in local or regional stores. Suggest ways the book can be promoted.

Keep in mind that chain buyers are often very difficult to reach by telephone, and that chain stores are generally the least likely to purchase books that are self-published or published by small presses. Sometimes chains will purchase these books only if they can order them from a wholesaler.

The Publishers Marketing Association has a program in which members may participate. For a fee, your book can be submitted to a jury that selects self-published and small-press books for presentation each season to the major chain buyers. Contact PMA for details.

Direct Marketing

Direct marketing can be a good way to get initial sales of a book that has trouble finding retail distribution. It can also be extremely profitable.The key to direct marketing is finding an efficient, targeted way to reach the specific audience that is most interested in your book. For example, a book for special needs children might not be of interest to general retailers, but could sell well to the parents of these children.You might reach them through advertising in the appropriate publication, or by mailing to a list of parents of special children, or to professionals who work with them.

Direct Mail

Consider buying, renting, or creating a mailing list of potential book buyers who may be particularly interested in your book. Send them a letter or simple flyer advertising your book. Include a self-addressed envelope for them to use if they would like to order a copy of the book. If your budget allows it, make the envelope postage-paid.

Mailing lists are available through mailing list brokers who can usually tailor a list to meet very detailed specifications. There are also specialists like Market Data Retrieval and QED who offer teacher and library lists. Other special interest lists can be purchased through associations listed in the directory.

Keep in mind that direct marketing is a science that takes time to master. Proceed with caution, testing the smallest possible mailing to any given list, to determine whether the list is truly responsive to what you have to offer, and to be certain that your mail piece is effective, before spending substantial sums on printing and postage.

Also be aware that timing is critical to a successful direct mail campaign. Consumers make the vast majority of their book purchases at the holidays. Educators are accustomed to buying at the beginning of the school year and in early spring.

Advertising

Consider placing an advertisement for your book in local parenting or special interest publications. Choose the timing of your ad carefully, and stick to very targeted, low-cost media. Remember that hardcover and picture books sell particularly well during the Christmas season and that young adult books are often bought by teens, not parents.

Keep in mind that unless your advertisement includes a special offer or strong call to action, it may not generate sales. Include a time-limited coupon to encourage readers to respond.

Rather than trying to sell your book directly to the public through advertising, you may want to consider offering to participate with a bookseller, sharing the cost of an ad in the local paper or in the bookstore newsletter

Special Sales

Selling large quantities of books at a specially negotiated price is called Special Sales. It involves selling books through non-retail and institutional outlets. These can include book clubs, book fairs, premium sales, and catalogs. Large publishing houses have special sales departments. Smaller houses may handle special sales through the marketing department.

Sometimes this requires selling quantities of the book to another company at discounted rates for resale. Or it may involve selling that company the rights to print a quantity of books under its own imprint for resale, while you receive a royalty.

Unless you or your agent have contracted to retain rights for you to sell to a specific market, you should start by talking with the person in charge of special sales at your publishing house.

If the idea you have is to sell to a catalog company, corporation, association, specialty store, or other outlet with which the publisher already deals, you may be asked to simply share any information you have that would help make a sale. If you want to pursue a lead in an area the publisher does not cover, you can discuss who should make the contact and how far you should take negotiations.

You should start by writing to the special sales manager, outlining your marketing ideas. These can be the names and addresses of contacts that you would like the publisher to consider making, or ways that you would like to supplement the publisher's special sales activities. If you don't get a response, wait a few weeks, then contact the publisher again to find out if there are plans to act on your ideas. If not, ask what you can do yourself.

The publisher may ask you to contact the vendor to see whether there is interest, then turn over negotiations to the special sales department, or you may be asked to proceed in some other way.

Book Clubs

Once your book has a proven sales record, you may want to send a copy with reviews of the book for consideration to age-appropriate home or school book clubs. Home book clubs sell directly by mail to children and parents. School clubs sell to students in grades K-12 through brochures distributed by teachers.

The major school book clubs are run by Scholastic. The directory lists grade levels for each.

Premium Sales

Recommend the book as a premium to marketers of related products. For example, if you have written a children's cookbook, Pillsbury might purchase a quantity for resale through an advertisement on bags of Pillsbury flour.

Catalog Sales

Check the *Directory of Mail Order Catalogs* to find out which catalogs may be most appropriate for your book. Don't forget that museum, toy, and gift catalogs can be ideal for picture books. There are a number of children's toy catalogs, such as Hearthsong and Toys to Grow On, that sell children's books. Chinaberry offers a catalog and on-line store of quality children's and teen books and audio. Buyers for these outlets will probably need to see a sample before placing an order.

Also, keep in mind that companies may do an expanded gift catalog for the holiday season and that many special interest groups put out catalogs. So, the National Wildlife Federation might want to know about a book on an endangered species. Ordering information for the catalog directory is at the back of this book. You may wish to check whether your local library or direct marketing association has a copy you can use.

Acting as Your Own Distributor

Your publisher may be willing to set you up as a distributor. You would then buy your books at an agreed-upon discount and resell them in bulk at a profit. The publisher benefits from having an expert on the subject selling quantities of books, and you get more money than you would have received through royalties alone. You can take a case of your books with you to offer whenever you speak to a group, or visit a new city where you may discover a specialty bookstore that would do well with your book.

Subrights

One effective way to gain attention for your book is to get it excerpted in an appropriately targeted magazine. Normally, a magazine contracts with the publisher and pays a fee for rights to reprint a portion of the book. If the magazine buys first serial rights, it can run the excerpt in advance of the book's publication. Second serial rights are for excerpts printed after the book is published. Another way for the magazine or newspaper to gain rights to use a part of a book is if the publisher or author decides to grant those rights without charge for publicity purposes.

One approach to publicizing non-fiction books is to identify information that magazines and newspapers may want to reprint and to allow the editor the option to use that material as long as proper credit is given to the book, author, and publisher.

Another way to promote read-aloud storybooks is to send them to producers of children's radio programs who can dramatize them on the air. If, in addition, your publisher is willing to donate several free copies, you may be able to get some good on-air promotion from the radio station.

Be sure to check with your publisher or your agent before giving permission for broadcast or reprint use of your book, to make sure that you own the right to do so.

CHAPTER III

The School and Library Markets

The percentage of children's and young adult titles sold to the educational market is significant and at times has surpassed the volume sold through retail channels. In recent years over $648 million was spent on children's and young adult books in school and public libraries.

The diverse educational market is represented by public libraries, school libraries and media centers, and classrooms. These three segments purchase trade hardcover and paperback books, as well as nonfiction titles usually published in series that are used for homework support. Prebound books are another type of book purchased by libraries and classrooms. Libraries select appropriate books for their collections by reading reviews, relying on sample copies provided by publishers or wholesalers, and considering titles pre-selected by their wholesalers, and then announced in various publications the wholesaler makes available to their customers. Classroom teachers may buy from specialty wholesalers or bookstores — many bookstores give teachers a discount on purchases.

It may be that your book is most appropriate for libraires and classrooms and won't really sell through retail channels. In this case, there are many ways you can help promote your book.

Review Journals and Professional Publications

It is important to realize that teachers and librarians rely heavily on review journals such as *Booklist*, *School Library*

Journal, *Horn Book Magazine*, *Kirkus Reviews* and *VOYA* (for young adult books), and professional magazines such as *Book Links*, *Learning*, *Instructor*, *Curriculum Connections* and *Teaching K-8* for recommendations on new books to purchase. *Foreword* and *Multicultural Review* are important niche journals that also review children's books. Many institutions allocate limited acquisition funds by requiring that a book be reviewed before it can be purchased.

It's critical to get your book reviewed in these periodicals. In most cases, your publisher will submit your book; but if not, or if you have self-published your book, you can submit it yourself. Send it to the Children's Book Editor at the journal; most have web sites where you can find submission guidelines. Most of these journals only review hardcover books, but check the submission guidelines for detailed information.

If your book receives a positive review, be sure to quote the journal in any promotional or publicity material and on the book jacket, if possible.

Educational Wholesalers

Most schools and libraries do their book purchasing through wholesalers, so it is important to make your book available through these sources. Baker & Taylor is the largest wholesaler to the public library market. Book Wholesalers, Inc., Brodart Co. and Ingram Book Company also service public libraries. The largest wholesaler to the school library market is Follett Library Resources, however Baker and Taylor, Brodart and Ingram also service school libraries.

Many institutions prefer to purchase hardcovers; if your book is available only in paperback you may still be able to sell it through a rebinder. These companies, such as Permabound Books and Sagebrush Education Resources, buy selected paperbacks in bulk, rebind them as hardcovers, and sell them exclusively to classrooms, school libraries and public libraries.

Some educational wholesalers focus on selling to classrooms. They stock large inventories of paperback books and focus on selling classroom sets to schools. The Educational Paperback Association (EPA) is a good source of information about wholesalers and publishers for the educational markets.

Promoting Your Book to Educators and Schools

The first step you must take before approaching the school market is deciding whether your book is appropriate and, if so, for what age group. You can discuss this with the publisher or you can talk to local teachers if you are unsure. Once you have determined this, you can develop a marketing plan, which may include developing a targeted mailing list, visiting schools and giving book talks, writing and distributing a teacher's guide for your book, and attending local or national teacher's conferences.

Mailing List

If you would like to begin doing school visits and promoting your book to teachers, it may be helpful to develop a special email or snail mail teacher's mailing list. This is an excellent way to let teachers know when your book has won an award or garnered a positive review, inform them about the new teacher's guide you've created, or let them know when you are planning a visit to their area and would be available for a school visit.

School Visits

Schools are often pleased to have authors visit, as a way to inspire students to read. The best place to begin arranging author appearances is in your own community. Teachers are likely to be interested in local celebrities and will appreciate not having to pay travel costs. If your book is for young children, visit local child care centers and offer to read to the children, or donate a book to be read at story hour. This could generate sales to parents.

If you grew up or went to school in another area, consider contacting your grade, middle, or high school alma mater. You are almost certain to get a warm welcome.

Ask teachers, area reading specialists, and professors at local teacher's colleges if they would be interested in having you talk with their students about writing. Also consider speaking at colleges that offer children's literature classes. You could offer to teach a writing class.

Contact schools in cities or regions that feature prominently in your book, or relate in some way to its subject matter. You may also want to check *Chase's Calendar of Events*, a book that lists regional events. Write to schools in those communities and ask if you can get involved in local events.

Develop a special presentation based on your book. To help explain your presentation, develop a separate promotional brochure that explains how your program could fit into a classroom environment or relate to thematic or topical areas of study.

Planning and Giving a Book Talk

Anyone who has spoken to a class of fourth graders can tell you that this is not an audience to be taken lightly. The key is to know as much about your audience and the format of the program as possible before you plan your talk. Ask teachers in advance whether there are special topics they would like you to address during your visit. Then make sure you are well-prepared to give an informative and entertaining presentation.

Contact the teacher two months before your school visit to suggest that she order books for you to autograph during your visit. Ask that the students read your book and prepare questions in advance. It will make your visit much more fun and meaningful for everyone involved.

Outline and practice your presentation so you know what points you will cover and can speak without reading from notes. You may want to keep an outline or note cards to refer to while you talk.

Use visuals, such as a flip chart, slides, PowerPoint, or even samples of book jackets or a manuscript to help your audience stay interested in the topic. Entertain listeners with anecdotes or stories that help illustrate your points.

Give your audience plenty of opportunities to participate in the discussion. For example, in discussing the writing process, you might want to start a story and have students tell you what should come next in the plot, or how one of the characters would react to a situation. Or you might want to give them an opportunity to edit a paragraph with spelling errors or inconsistencies to show what an editor does with a book.

Leave time for questions and comments from the audience. Try to give anyone who wants to ask a question the chance to talk at least once. When you are preparing to close, announce that you can only take a few more questions, so that no one is slighted.

Creating Your Own Teacher's Guide

Some publishers offer short guides to books that have been adopted for classroom use. The books can be fiction or non-fiction and guides will vary according to the type of book and the publisher's own style (many examples of teacher's guides can be found on publisher's web sites).

Teacher's guides generally include a brief synopsis of the story, a list of suggested topics for classroom discussion, and ideas for classroom and extracurricular activities that can stem from book discussions. They are usually one to two pages in length, unless the guide covers several of the author's titles or a book series.

If your book has gained acceptance in the schools, you may want to consider writing a guide to your book that you can give to teachers. If you tailor your copy to fit your publisher's format and style, your publisher may be willing to print copies of your guide and add your title to the list of guides offered. The web site *TeachingBooks.net* has links to thousands of published teacher guides and is an excellent resource for studying what guides are available.

When creating a guide, be sure to talk with a teacher at the appropriate grade level. She can tell you if your ideas are feasible and may have some creative suggestions as well.

If your book is a picture book, create a guide that focuses on activities and games relating to the format or subject of your book. Teacher's guides for middle grade and young adult books should emphasize discussion questions, research projects, and suggestions for activities both in and out of the classroom.

The following page is a sample teacher's guide for a picture book, reproduced with permission from Clarion Books/ Houghton Mifflin Company.

Sample Teacher's Guide (page 1)

A Teacher's Guide

Vote!

written and illustrated by Eileen Christelow

- Teaching Extensions and Activities
- Discussion Questions
- Word Search
- Resources

Using a town's mayoral election as a model, this lively, information-packed book covers all aspects of the voting process, from campaigning and debating to registering and volunteering, all the way to the voting booth. There's even a recount! *Vote!*, which was vetted by an expert in voter education, includes a timeline of the history of voting in the United States, a glossary of words associated with voting, a discussion of American political parties, and a list of Internet resources.

"It's hard to imagine a more accessible introduction to voting." — ALA *Booklist,* starred review

Teaching Extensions and Activities

1. *Vote!* focuses on a mayoral election. Ask your students to imagine they are running for the mayor's office. Have them write about the problems confronting their community. Discuss the difference between issues that are important to them personally and issues that are important to many different people.

2. Each student can design a campaign poster using poster board, paints, and markers. Decorate your classroom with the finished posters.

3. Ask your city or town's mayor to speak to your class about what a mayor does after he or she is elected. Students can submit questions beforehand that should focus on the issues the class has identified in number 1.

4. Make flashcards of the words in the glossary of *Vote!*. Draw one card at a time and ask students to use the new word in a sentence.

5. Ask students to name the different symbols and pictures used in election campaigns: Uncle Sam, the stars and stripes, the political party symbols, etc. Let them design political buttons to wear. (An easy method is to cut circles from poster board and affix Velcro dots.)

6. Ask students to write to their state representatives about a local issue of importance to them. Mail the letters and keep track of the responses.

www.houghtonmifflinbooks.com 1 of 4

Sample Teacher's Guide (page 2)

7. Political parties are an important aspect of the political system in the United States. *Vote!* includes a section titled "More About Political Parties." Divide your class into three sections: the "Monkeys," who want bananas for a snack; the "Choconuts," who want chocolate milk for snacktime; and a smaller group of undecideds. Have the two parties debate in order to try to convince the undecideds to join their party.

8. The "Timeline of Voting Rights" gives an accurate snapshot of who in this country could vote when. You can have your students participate in an exercise that will personalize this timeline for them.

- Ask all students to stand on one side of the room. Then say, "In 1788 only white men who owned land and paid taxes could vote. If you were an adult then, could you have voted? If you could have, then step over to the other side of the room." Continue forward through the timeline.
- "In 1913 women living in Wyoming, Washington, California, Arizona, Kansas, Oregon, and Illinois could vote. As an adult, could you have voted?"
- "In 1920 the Nineteenth Amendment made it possible for all women to vote. As an adult, could you have voted?"
- "In 1965 the Voting Rights Act made it possible for African Americans to vote without fear of being hurt or killed. As an adult, could you have voted safely now?"
- "In 1975 the Voting Rights Act also included protections for Hispanic, Asian, and Native American citizens. As an adult, could you have voted safely now?"
- Is everyone standing on the other side of the room? What did it feel like to be one of the last people to walk over to the other side of the room? Discuss equal voting rights with the students in your classroom.

Discussion Questions

1. Voting is a way to choose. Talk about different ways you vote every day. Does your family vote on where to take a vacation? Do you vote about which movie to watch? How do you decide where to eat if you want pizza and your sister wants chicken fingers?

2. Does anyone in the class know someone in their family who has been elected? To what office? What do they do?

3. Why do you think it took so long for all women to be able to vote?

4. The leader in the United States is called the president. What are leaders in some other countries called?

www.houghtonmifflinbooks.com 2 of 4

Promoting Your Book to Librarians and Libraries

Your marketing plan for targeting libraries might include developing or purchasing a targeted mailing list, participating in programs at your local library, and attending local or national library conferences.

Mailing List

It might be useful to develop a mailing list of librarians, so that you can let them know when you have a new book, notify them of awards or positive reviews, or let them know when you will be doing a school visit in their community. You can also purchase mailing lists from the American Library Association that target public libraries with large children's collections.

If your book appeals to a special interest group, find out which libraries have related special collections. See if they would carry your book. A good source book is *The American Library Directory.*

Working With Your Local Library

Get to know your local librarian and ask whether you can participate in programs sponsored by the library. Activities can include reading aloud from your work at a children's story hour, giving formal presentations to parents and teachers, or participating in programs to help raise money for the library, such as a "Meet the Author" luncheon.

You can also ask the librarian about community or regional programs, such as "reading roundtable" groups in your area. Volunteer to work with the library to run programs featuring local authors. Discuss the kinds of programs in which you would be willing to participate and stay in touch periodically to offer your services.

Donate a copy of your book to the local library. They may or may not choose to add it to their collection, but at least the librarian will know about the book in case a patron is interested.

National Education and Library Conventions

Attending conventions is an excellent way to learn about the institutional market and to get your name known. The American Library Association (ALA), The American Booksellers Association (ABA), The National Council of Teachers of English (NCTE), and The International Reading Association (IRA) all have annual conferences that feature authors and illustrators.

As a new writer or illustrator, you'll initially attend national conferences at your own expense. Once there, meet librarians and educators and collect names to add to your mailing list. Ask your publisher to schedule time for you to autograph books at their booth.

Find out whether there will be a trade show daily newspaper or a convention directory that will list events. Contact the editor to advise her of your autographing.

Create a handout for teachers and librarians that includes a biographical profile, a description of your book, and information on the type of presentations you can give at schools and meetings. Provide the name and number of the publicity contact at your publishing house and information on how you can be reached directly.

Local/Regional Education and Library Conventions

Local chapters of the national education and library associations run conferences throughout the year. You may want to attend or participate in these events.

You can obtain information on scheduled meetings by contacting your state education and library associations or by contacting the national headquarters of the IRA, NCTE, ALA and other groups listed in the directory. Most of these organizations offer websites with current information on conferences. Contact coordinators of any conferences that will be held in your area and offer to be a guest on a panel.

Talk with your publisher about the possibility of running a booth at a local conference or meeting. This may give the publisher the chance to distribute catalogs and promotional material at a meeting they had not planned to attend. It will give you an opportunity to showcase your book.

Never throw out a name. If you keep track of the people you meet at conventions and at schools and libraries you visit, you can send them notices about future books. Always carry a supply of business cards so you can tell people how to reach you.

CHAPTER IV

Bookstore Promotion

Bookstores are always looking for in-store events to attract parents and children. There are many ways for you to work with local independent bookstores and children's specialty bookstores to promote your book.

A good source of information on children's only bookstores and stores with strong children's sections is the Association of Booksellers for Children. ABC has a mailing list of member bookstores for promotional use. As an author, you are eligible to become an associate member.

Getting Started

Any children's only bookstore is an excellent place to promote your book.

Stop in and talk with the store owner about the kinds of events that go on in the store. Discuss whether you might participate and how your book can be featured. Most likely, the owner or manager will also be able to tell you about other book-related events in your area.

Ask if you can conduct a story hour to read aloud from your book. If the bookseller is not willing to purchase a quantity of the book to start, you may want to purchase copies of the book yourself and offer the store a commission on sales.

Book Signings

The advantages of doing bookstore appearances generally outweigh the disadvantages.The advantages include helping to sell more books in the local community and gaining additional publicity. By doing store appearances you will develop relationships with store owners and employees who are in a position to recommend your books — not only to consumers, but also to teachers and librarians.

Ask whether the store is willing to have a book signing event for your book. If so, unless you have an active publicity department behind you, you should plan to do much more than simply show up at the appointed hour.Whether you are self-published or not, your book signing will be more fun for everyone, and more successful, if you invest some time and energy in preparation and in helping out the bookseller.

Many authors who have done bookstore appearances will tell you that the downside is that you can never tell how many people will show up.With that in mind, authors should make sure to help stores draw crowds.

Working with Your Bookseller Host

Booksellers will nearly always welcome your help and suggestions. Even though it's more work for you, consider creating a "promotion package" that booksellers could borrow from you to announce your store visit.The promotion package can be done inexpensively and can include items that are reusable, so you can change the date and time listed for each occasion.This could be offered on loan to stores where you are going to do a signing.You can also ask if there are other ways for you to help promote your signing. For example, you should invite your friends!

The promotion package could include special signs for the window and front of the store, a box containing window display materials appropriate to the subject of the book, and one or more easel-backed signs to set up at the register or on tables. You could also enclose a list of your previous books, biographical material, and several prints of your publicity photo.

The idea is to offer a service in advance rather than just trying to fill a gap at the last minute. Not every bookseller will take you up on your offer, but those who do will probably get a better response and will remember you when you offer to come back.

A number of children's bookstores send newsletters to their customers. Be sure to plan any event so there is enough time to list your visit in the store newsletter and to send out promotional flyers.

Find out what publicity the bookseller plans to do. If necessary, supplement the bookseller's effort by sending announcements to local newspapers and radio stations to get your appearance listed on event calendars. If the event is newsworthy, call editors to offer to do press interviews. You or the bookseller should also notify area librarians and reading teachers, who may bring groups to the event.

If store owners realize you are willing to help make their events successful, they are more likely to have you back in the future and the relationship may have long-term benefits for you both.

Special In-Store Programs

One way to draw a good crowd to a bookstore is to go beyond a basic autograph session and develop a special program that ties into the theme of your book. For example, if you have a Halloween book, you could do a pumpkin-carving workshop. Consider whether your book's topic could relate to a holiday or theme promotion and talk with the bookseller about your idea for an in-store event that is appropriate.

Be very careful about suggesting events for the Christmas season. That is the busiest time of the year for most retailers and it is unlikely that they will be interested in running events during that period. However, if your book is topical, you could always offer to design a window or in-store display featuring your book and related books on the same topic.

All the guidelines for a successful book signing apply to creating a successful special event. And the advance preparation that is required is even greater!

CHAPTER V

Special Promotions

Awards

Do enter your book in state and national book award competitions. But first check with your publisher, so you can avoid duplication of efforts.

A number of children's book awards are listed in this book's Directory. The Children's Book Council's *Awards and Prizes* is a comprehensive database, available online at *www.cbcbooks.org*. Also check the awards listing in *Literary Market Place,* the annual reference guide to the book publishing industry. You can check each award's web site for submission guidelines.

Museums

Contact children's and other museums that may be interested in your book to find out about events in which you can participate.

Approach museum shop managers to find out whether they will carry your book in the store. Many museum stores have been expanding their children's book sections in recent years because museum patrons are often buyers of high-end picture and gift books.

The Museum Store Association, which is listed in the directory, rents a list of museum store buyers. You may also want to contact the American Association of Museums, which sells lists of museum directors' names, categorized by type of museum.

Community Organizations and Tourist Attractions

Involvement in community organizations can lead to speaking engagements that generate book sales. The local chamber of commerce and tourist bureau are good places to start. Also talk with the directors of area community centers and tourist attractions.

Notify your chamber of commerce and the local tourist bureau that you are a local author and are willing to participate in local events that may be sponsored by businesses or tourist attractions.

Offer an autographed copy of your book as a prize for area contests or fund-raisers. For example, your community center may sponsor a children's Halloween party and give books as prizes for the best costumes. This will help promote you as a local author and generate interest in the book.

If your book is about animals, contact the local zoo to find out about upcoming events at which you or your book can be featured.

Select an appropriate tourist attraction in your area, such as an amusement park. Offer to donate a quantity of free books to be given to the first 50 or 100 children that visit on a certain day. This can be done in return for promotion and publicity.

Non-profit and Special Interest Groups

Working with non-profit and special interest groups can provide access to an appropriate audience that would otherwise be unaware of your book. Group members may be especially receptive to offers that are associated with the organization. Working with such organizations can often generate much more publicity than an independent promotion of a children's book.

A topical book can be effectively marketed to associations that have a special interest in the subject. This is particularly true of non-fiction titles, but can work for fiction, too, if your book is factually based.

Start by contacting the publicity department of any organization you have used as a source in writing your book. Ask about services they provide for their members and for outsiders needing information on the subject. They may be willing to include your book in their reference library or on a recommended reading list. For example, you might contact the Office of Indian Education if your book is about Native Americans.

Find out whether an organization publishes bibliographies of recommended books; has a hotline or information service that refers callers to source material; gives awards for topical books; hosts an annual conference that showcases related products; or sells mailing lists that you can buy for direct marketing purposes. Consider sending complimentary copies of the book to the president or other key members of the organization. They may be willing to endorse or refer others to the book. If you can claim special expertise in explaining how to present the information to children, ask whether you could be considered as a guest speaker at regional or national conferences.

You are likely to find that some organizations are more receptive than others, but if your book relates closely to what they do, it is likely that the contact will prove worthwhile. In addition to organizations that you may have discovered in researching your book, you can check your local library for the *Encyclopedia of Associations*.

Offer to donate a percentage of royalties from books sold during a specific period to a related charity. In return, the charity should provide promotional support. Find out whether your publisher will match your donation.

Religious Groups

Books don't need a religious theme to cross over into the religious market. Picture books and stories about family and values can sell well through religious outlets, catalogs and direct mail. Books with a religious theme, or by an author who is known in a particular religious community, will find a natural home here.

If your book is of interest to a particular religious group, talk with local religious leaders to find out whether it can be used in an affiliated school or library. You may also want to attend association conventions or get on a panel to discuss religious children's books or other topics.

Contact national associations that might consider your book for review or bibliographic listings. Contact associations like the Christian Booksellers Association, the Jewish Book Council, the Catholic Library Association, and the National Catholic Education Association to find out about specialty distributors, stores, libraries, and other outlets that may be interested in carrying your book.

Many materials are sold to Sunday schools and individuals interested in religious materials via direct mail and special interest catalogs. Contact a list broker (see special sales) for possible lists, and check the *Directory of Mail Order Catalogs*.

CHAPTER VI

Publicity

Every book has unique elements that can be used to generate publicity. You may focus on subject matter, the setting in which the story takes place, the style of illustration, the author, or the illustrator. The key is to identify those qualities that make your book special and use that information to devise a strategy for publicity.

Publicity can include a wide range of activities, and many ideas featured in this book can be considered publicity ideas. This section focuses on gaining publicity through television, radio, and print media.

If your book is not self-published, remember to talk with your publisher's publicity department or children's book marketing manager to find out what work has already been done on your book. You do not want to duplicate work the publisher has already done, or confuse media contacts by making unnecessary phone calls. Also, by meeting with and discussing your ideas with the publicist or marketing manager, you can find out how your time can most effectively be spent.

Creating Your Own Press Package

A basic press kit publicizing a new book generally consists of a "pitch" letter designed to get an editor excited about the book, a press release explaining why the book is newsworthy, and an author biography. It can also include additional information, such as a biographical profile of the illustrator or a sheet of interesting tips, quotations, or facts from the book. More elaborate kits are likely to include these elements plus material of interest to a particular editor or producer. For example, discussion questions in a Q-and-A format can be helpful to television and radio producers for on-air conversation. Tip sheets and trivia are ideal for smaller magazines and newspapers who work on a tight schedule and like to have extra material on hand in case they need to fill space at the last minute. Surveys, topical articles, and statistics can provide media contacts with the angles they need to build an interesting subject into a feature story.

While a press kit can provide an editor or producer with a variety of story angles, a well-written pitch letter explaining why a book and author should be of interest to a particular editor can go a long way. If it is the only item going out with a book, the pitch letter should include a paragraph that explains why the book is newsworthy and at least a few sentences about the author's and/or illustrator's background. Be sure to include your web site address, if you have one.

Send a copy to your publisher's publicity department and use the material to publicize the book yourself.

Writing Press Releases

Feature the most interesting and important aspect of your book in the headline and lead paragraph. Try to convey the tone of the book in the release. An effective release is factual, yet interesting, well-written, and engaging, like a good news story. It includes all pertinent information, such as the age of the intended audience, and background information on the author and illustrator. Substantiate your release with quotes from the review media or other objective third parties whenever possible.

- All releases should be typed and double-spaced.
- Provide a contact name and telephone number at the top of the press release for easy reference.

- List the book title, publisher, and date of publication at the bottom of the release.
- Specify whether the book is fiction or nonfiction and if it is available in hardcover and paperback editions.
- List prices and ISBN numbers, if appropriate, for all editions.

Sample Press Release

Raab
associates, inc.

345 Millwood Rd • Chappaqua, NY 10514
914.241.2117 • www.raabassociates.com

FOR IMMEDIATE RELEASE:

Contact: Joyce Stein
info@raabassociates.com

Newly Revised Primer on Self-Promotion Published for Children's Book Authors and Illustrators

As the number of children's book publishers and publishing options has increased, authors and illustrators have had to work harder to make their books stand out from the crowd.

Now, Raab Associates Inc. will publish the tenth revised and updated edition of ***An Author's Guide to Children's Book Promotion,*** by Susan Salzman Raab. This marketing primer for authors and illustrators of children's and young adult books presents suggestions for marketing to bookstores, schools, libraries, and online venues. It includes information on publicity, promotion, special sales, self-publishing, and the Internet. The book also provides a directory of key organizations, awards, reference books, and trade magazines.

An Author's Guide to Children's Book Promotion is a must for any children's book author, whether she wants to market and sell a self-published book, or discover new ways to work with her publisher to help promote front- and back-list titles.

A specialist in children's book marketing, Susan Salzman Raab is co-owner of Raab Associates Inc., a public relations, marketing and direct marketing agency. She has worked at Scholastic, Dell and Bantam. She is the marketing advisor to the Society of Children's Book Writers and Illustrators (SCBWI) and writes the "To Market" column for their publication *The Bulletin.* For more information visit www.raabassociates.com

###

An Author's Guide to Children's Book Promotion
(Nonfiction)
Written by Susan Salzman Raab
Price: $14.95 paperback, 10th edition
ISBN: 09621211-7-7
Publication Date: April 2007 (revised and updated)

Building Media Lists

Create a media list of producers at television and radio stations and editors at daily and weekly newspapers and regional magazines who may have an interest in local celebrities or children's books. You can compile a basic list from your telephone book and the local newspaper. For more detailed information on local and national media, use one of the media directories listed at the back of this book.

The smaller the town in which you live, and the fewer authors there are in your area, the easier it will be to get local publicity.Don't forget the neighborhood sections of newspapers and the state and regional editors at major newspapers. They are often receptive to stories on local personalities. Contact the public affairs department at local newspapers, television, and radio stations to find out whether they can mention events in which you will be participating on their events calendar.

Send a press release on your book to organizations with which you are or have been affiliated that will be interested in your activities. Examples are alumni newspapers, church or synagogue newsletters, and home town newspapers. Make sure you include a personal note to the editor regarding your relationship to the organization or community.

Also, remember that most people in business read journals relating to their field. These journals often include short news items on people in the industry. For example, if you run a drycleaner, you might send a letter to the editor of American Drycleaner telling him about your newly published children's book. Be sure to include information on your background and your business.

Create a media list of education, family, or children's book editors at state and local newspapers and send them a copy of the book and a press release telling them about the book and that you are a local author.

Compile or rent a list of book reviewers at newspapers across the country. A mailing list can be rented from Bacon's Mailing Services, which is listed in the directory. Send reviewers a self-addressed stamped envelope and a reply card that they can use to request copies of your book for review. Include space for them to check if and when they review children's books. Use the sample media reply card, on the next page, as a guide.

If your book is appropriate for school-age children, compile a list of review editors at educational publications like *Booklist* and *School Library Journal* that should receive copies of your book. Check with your publisher first to make sure you are not duplicating mailings.

Send books and press releases to parenting publications locally and nationally, particularly if your book is for young children. There are regional parenting papers as well as national publications like *Parents Magazine*, *Child Magazine*, *Family Fun* and *Parenting*. There are also many good parenting sites on the Internet that you can pursue. To obtain a list of regional parenting papers, contact Parenting Publications of America (PPA).

Sample Media Reply Card

Dear ___________:

I am compiling a list of book reviewers who are interested in receiving children's books for review. Please take a moment to check below to indicate your interest and return in the enclosed self-addressed stamped envelope. Thank you.

I would like to receive children's books for review:

___yes ___no

If yes: Approximately how many books do you review each year? ______

Please indicate the frequency with which you would like to receive children's books. Check more than one, if applicable:

____ Prior to publication

____ For a Winter Holiday Roundup

____ For Children's Book Week in November

____ Other, please explain

____

____

____

How many months in advance would you like to receive a review copy? __________

Send the book and press materials to publications that reach the appropriate age of readers. For example, information on a book of interest to teenage girls would go to *YM*, the teen magazine, and a topical book for younger children would go to *YAK'S Corner*, a newspaper insert for kids.

Books should always be sent by the publisher to the book trade media, which includes *Publishers Weekly* and the ABA's *Bookselling This Week*.

Arrange telephone interviews with radio stations across the country that feature authors or discuss issues of interest to parents. Send the book and press materials to radio and television stations with programming that appeals directly to children. Radio Disney is a network that is known nationally, but there are also shows that broadcast locally.

Make sure to customize your cover letter for the different mailing lists. You can send the same letter to producers and editors on the same list.

It's important to develop and maintain an up-to-date mailing list and to keep records of conversations. You can keep this on a computer database, but an index card file can also work well. The basics are the contact's name, job title, organization name, address, phone, fax, e-mail and web site addresses. In addition, you could include the type of audience the publication or station reaches, its circulation or audience size, the kind of books your contact does and doesn't want to see, the books sent in the past, the date on which you last spoke to that person, and when you want to call the person again. You may also want to include relevant personal information, such as whether the contact has young children.

You may want to keep some of the same information on contacts you've made at associations, booksellers, people you've met at industry conventions, and individuals at your publishing house. Publishing is a tightly knit community and people move around frequently, so past contacts can often be useful at a later date. It's also to your benefit to help your contacts by putting them in touch with others who may be interested in what they are doing, or by relaying information that they may find useful.

Pitching the Story to the Media

For the best publicity results, call the stations and publications when you are developing your lists to make sure that you are sending information to the appropriate person. Don't count on anyone forwarding material for you.

Don't wait for editors to call you. The only way to generate interest is to make a personal appeal, so plan time for follow-up calls. Expect that it will take several calls to each contact to get an answer. Follow-up calls should start within a week of the person receiving the material. If you wait too long, your contacts probably won't have or remember the information.

Be prepared for every call with a brief statement saying who you are, what was included in the package, and why you thought they would be interested in the story. Be sure to remind them of any previous conversations.

If one of your contacts is receptive, try to arrange an interview as soon as possible. You don't want to take a chance, by waiting, that a reporter will drop yours for another story idea.

Keep good notes on who you have talked to and their interests. It is possible that someone who can't do a story now may be willing to talk with you about another angle or a new book at some future date. It is also important not to anger someone who has no interest by calling again with the same question. If the producer or editor is not interested, ask about other people in their organization who might want to talk with you.

Sometimes you can interest an editor by customizing a story to meet her needs. For example, she may not want to profile you and your book alone, but might consider a story on a group of local authors. If you can package that kind of story for a producer or editor, she will be more willing to talk with you the next time you approach her with an idea. Before deciding to invest time in packaging a story, make sure to ask the producer or editor if she expects to be able to mention you and your book.

Timing

The best times to publicize a children's book are just prior to publication and in time for the Winter Holiday season. Children's Book Week, which is sponsored each November by the Children's Book Council, is another good occasion.

- Stories in monthly magazines are often scheduled five or six months in advance.
- Television shows can also require several months' notice.
- Radio programming, weekly magazines, and newspapers are more flexible, but usually want at least several weeks to prepare a story.

Radio and Television

Getting radio and television coverage for children's books is usually harder than placing magazine and newspaper stories. One reason is that producers have had less experience with children's book authors and they don't want to take the chance on a guest who will "freeze up" on the air.They may also worry that the show's host will be less conversant when talking about a children's book. Some will rule out the idea completely because the topic is considered "too soft," "not newsworthy," "for too young an audience," or "not sexy enough."The trick is to find shows that are more flexible, and to learn to position yourself and your books to overcome such objections.

First, consider whether your book ties into what's going on in the news, or to a trend. If so, write a press release and pitch letter that emphasize how your book provides a unique angle on that subject. If your book is not topical, it may have elements that can be used for "how-to" segments with tips for parents and kids. Another aspect to consider for television is how your book can be presented in a visually exciting way, such as traveling to local places where interesting research was done, or showing an illustrator using a unique art technique.

If you feel you have a story to pitch for radio or television, there are a number of ways to build a contact list. One is to check a media directory, such as the *Gebbie Press All-In-One Directory*, which includes radio and television listings; there are also specialized directories, such as those published by Bacon's, which list radio and television shows in more detail.

Another cost-effective way to try to get radio and television coverage is to place an ad in *Radio-TV Interview Reports*. For a few hundred dollars you can have a half-page write-up in this newsletter, which mails monthly to nearly 4,000 producers at radio and television stations.They will even help you write the copy.

The format allows for a headline, a black and white photo of you or your book, a descriptive paragraph about the book, and examples of topics you can discuss. Entries also include a brief author biography and information on whether you are available for telephone or in-person interviews.

Before deciding when to run the ad, consider the timing and the subject of the book. You can either have the ad run when the book is first published, or time it to a month when the topic will attract attention. For example, you may want to hold a book about baseball until just before the season starts.

Preparing for Radio Interviews

If you are to be interviewed on a local show, listen several times in advance to learn more about the show's format and the host's style of interviewing. Does the show focus on a single issue, or on the guest's career? Are guests allowed time to expand on points they would like to make, or will you be expected to give brief responses to questions? Does the show leave time for call-ins from listeners? Are guests interviewed alone or with other guests? Is the host prone to stirring controversy or asking tough questions? Who are the listeners at that time of day and what will interest them?

When you schedule the interview, ask whether it will be live or taped and find out what topics they expect to cover. If it is live, try to arrange to talk with the host for a few minutes in advance to establish a rapport before you go on the air. For a taped interview, keep in mind that portions may be cut. Tell the host which points you feel are most important, either during the interview, or at the conclusion of the taping.

Before going on the air, review your material and jot down notes of key points you want to make. Flag those pages of your book that include references or quotes you want to use. (Don't assume that your host will have a copy of your book on hand; bring your own!) Have a friend quiz you in advance to prepare for tough or tricky questions. Prepare a reply for questions to which you find it difficult to respond quickly and smoothly. Have a watch handy so you can pace yourself during the interview and keep a pad and pen within reach in case you want to make notes during the discussion.

Once you're on, be enthusiastic and informative. Take your cues from the host and be sensitive to his or her concerns. Don't treat the show as an advertising vehicle, but be sure to work the title of your book into your conversation. The host will probably include this information at the beginning of the show when introducing you, and also during the wrap-up at the end. Tell the host in advance if you would like to give out an ordering phone number on the air, or would like your website's address mentioned.

Preparing for Television Interviews

The guidelines for radio apply to television as well, with the large difference that the audience will be able to see you! Robin Cohn, President of Robin Cohn and Company, a media consulting company in New York City, provided the following tips.

What to wear? Clothes for television should be subdued. Stay away from stripes checks and bold prints. If you normally wear glasses, wear them for the interview. Don't let anything you are wearing distract from what you are saying.

Talk to the host and forget the camera is there. Try not to date what you're saying, especially if the show is being taped. If you mention that something happened "today," the story will not be accurate a week later and may be scrapped.

Don't assume the interviewer will stay on one specific topic. Be prepared to answer questions on other subjects as well. While children's books are not usually controversial, be prepared. Don't evade a tough question. Answer as directly as you can, put your position in the best light, and move on. Be concise. Give a short, direct answer first, then elaborate with details. If an outrageous accusation or incorrect statement is made, don't let it go unchallenged. Refute it politely, give a brief, positive explanation, then shift to the topic you want aired.

And last, but not least, try to say everything you feel or know about your subject in one sentence. Then fit it into 20 seconds. Practice your "sound-byte" with a tape recorder until you are comfortable. And then make sure that you find a way to include this information in your answer, so that you get your important points across no matter how short your allotted time is and no matter what the interviewer says or asks!

CHAPTER VII

Web Sites and Blogs

One of the most common questions authors and illustrators ask is "Do I need a web site?"

If you have published at least one children's book, and you want to promote that book in a relatively inexpensive way, or if you're an illustrator who hasn't yet been published, but would like to make your work easily viewable by potential publishers, then you should probably have a web site.

A few years ago, no one was really sure whether having an Internet site was worth the time and trouble, but now that the Internet has proved itself as a valuable research and promotional tool, it's worth serious consideration by authors and illustrators.

For one thing, educators and librarians are increasingly using the Internet for author research, to contact authors for classroom projects and to decide who to bring to school for events. You don't want to miss your chance to reach this important audience for children's books.

If you think you might want to have a web site, give yourself some time to think it through. What do you want to achieve with your web site? How will it get built? Who will write the content? Who will keep the site updated? What components would you like to include and why? Do you want to try and generate school visits? Are you willing to answer fan mail from children via email? Do you want to sell autographed copies of your book to people who visit your site?

One important way to help you visualize all of this is to visit lots of author/illustrator sites and take notes about what you like and don't like. If you spend some time doing this, it will quickly become apparent to you what you would like to do, and not do, with your own site.

Building a Web Site

Components

Once you have decided that you need a web site, here are the four components you need to find:

1. Domain name — you need to register a unique domain name for your site (*www.greatauthor.com*).
2. Web site host — you need to find a company that will host your web site for you. Think of the host as the "landlord" for your "home" on the internet — you pay them so that your site will be "live" on the internet and visible to visitors.
3. Content — you need to have content on your site — text, pictures, book covers, etc.
4. Programming — you, or someone else, needs to take your content and, using HTML programming, turn your content into your web site, so that everyone can see it. HTML is the special language of the Internet, and all sites must be written in that language so that your site looks the same to everyone who views it.

Web Site Options

There are a variety of ways to take these four components and create your web site. Here are four choices, along with the costs and considerations of each.

Do-It-Yourself, With a Template Site

Cost: $150-$250 per year

Time Frame: 1 day

Smartwriters.com offers authors and illustrators an inexpensive template program ($10/month) where, after you register, you can enter your information and be on the Internet quickly. Author Illustrator Source offers its members ($99/year) a free listing. Both are ways for authors/illustrators to put up an informational web site very quickly and inexpensively. (Many Internet providers, like AOL, Earthlink and Yahoo allow members to create free web sites, but the information you can present here is usually pretty limited.)

Advantages: the most inexpensive and quickest way to be represented on the internet; no HTML knowledge is required; you will have complete control over the content and when it is updated, and your site will be promoted along with the other sites hosted by the organization.

Disdvantages: you don't have any say over the format, in some cases, the templates could limit the content you want to provide or require you to post content that you don't wish to post, and you will be responsible for updating the information.

Do-It-Yourself, With Software or a Hosting Company

Cost: $200-$250/year

Time frame: 2 days

There are many software packages that allow you to design a web site without knowing any HTML at all (Microsoft FrontPage is one example). There are also hundreds of web hosting companies that have templates enabling you to set up a web site without knowing any HTML (*www.hostway.com* is one example). Most are simple enough that you could create your site in a single weekend.

Advantages: fairly inexpensive, you will have complete control over your content.

Disdvantages: will take time which you would rather spend on your writing/illustrating; you will have to find your own host; if it crashes, you will be the one who has to fix it; and it might not be as professional looking as you would like.

Friend, Relative or Spouse

Cost: Depends

Time Frame: Depends

You may know someone who builds web sites as a hobby, or is willing to invest the time to learn in order to design your site.

Advantages: this could be a very inexpensive way to build a site, depending on your arrangement with the friend, and you will have more time to write/illustrate.

Disdvantages: what if you don't like what they do? Beware of homemade-looking sites!

Hire a Web Site Designer

Cost: $350 and up to design, depending on the size of site you want, and $200/year and up to maintain.

Time frame: A month or more, depending on size and the designer's schedule.

Advantages: this is the best way to create a totally unique site that will be flexible and professional looking.

Disdvantages: most expensive way, you will have more upkeep costs, and it will take some research to find the best designer for your needs.

Web Site Content

What kinds of information should your site include? Here are some common pages that many authors/illustrators include (detailed below):

- About the author - biography and photos
- Booklist
- Contact Information
- Guest Book
- Frequently Asked Questions (FAQ's)
- Links
- School and Library Visits
- Travel Schedule
- Educator and Librarian Resources
- Book Ordering Information
- Writing Samples
- Autographed Copies
- Art for sale

Biography

Since many visitors are looking for information about you, it's important that your site include a biography. Some authors and illustrators use biographies written by their publishers (often used in author brochures and on the publisher's web site) but others write a more informal, chatty piece for their own site. In either case, photographs add an extra dimension, whether they are official photographs or informal family pictures.

Book List

You want to make sure that visitors find out about all of your books when they visit your site, so provide a complete book list with title, co-authors and illustrators, publisher, price, ISBN, annotation, awards/reviews, a cover image and availability. Authors with out-of-print books often list those too, along with a suggestion to "look for this at your library" or provide ordering information if the author or illustrator has any copies remaining. Be sure to incorporate any awards or positive review mentions in your book descriptions. If your award list is lengthy, it may be more impressive to have a separate Awards page.

Contact Information

If you are willing to read and reply to fan mail, provide an email link to yourself on your site. It's a great way to find out what teachers, librarians, booksellers and students are thinking about you and your books. It's also a way for other authors or even publishers to reach you. Some authors and illustrators collect emails inquiring about their out-of-print books, and pass them along to their publisher.

If you are not willing to answer emails, it's important to at least provide an address where your fans can write to you with questions or comments, or with requests for a school visit.

Guest Book

Having a guest book feature is useful in two ways: it can let you see just exactly who is visiting your site, and it can help you build your mailing list. If you're going to include this, you should make it clear that you will be adding them to your mailing list, and that you will not share their personal info with anyone else.

Frequently Asked Questions (FAQ's)

This is a section of your site where visitors can go to quickly see answers to their most common questions. Examples might be: "How do I contact you for a school visit?" "Is this title still in print?" "When is your next book coming out?"

Links

There are several categories of links you might consider having on your site.

- Trade, Publisher and Author/Illustrator links — Many authors and illustrators provide links to their publishers' sites, book and library trade association sites, other author and illustrator sites, and sites about writing for children. A big advantage to doing this is that often these sites will do a reciprocal link back to your site, helping to increase your site's traffic. Be sure to include links to other places related to your books, too - for example, if your book is available in an audio format, or your art has been used for a greeting card.
- Topical Site links — If you've just completed a book on dinosaurs, or written a historical fiction novel, you might want to link to sites where your readers can go for more information on the subjects.
- Personal Interest links — It can be fun for your site visitors to learn more about you by visiting links to sites you like, if you feel comfortable with it. You might link to a site that relates to a hobby (skiing, music) or to an organization you support (Animal Welfare League, Sierra Club).

School/Library Visits

If you are interested in doing guest appearances at schools and libraries, your web site can be very useful in promoting that service. You might describe your fee and charge for expenses, the kinds of presentations you do, talk length; preferred audience size, and whether you are willing to autograph books and do extra teacher workshops. Be sure to provide them with a way to contact either yourself or someone at your publisher for more information.

Travel Schedule

Some authors and illustrators post their professional travel schedules on their sites.This allows bookstores, libraries and schools to see when you are coming to their area and investigate whether or not they can "piggyback" on your visit to their area. It also allows parents, kids and other fans to see where they might come to meet you.

Educator and Librarian Resources

If you and/or your publisher have created teacher or activity guides for any of your books, you should definitely make them available for downloading from your site.This would be a good place for you to have suggestions available for ways to use your book in the classroom; how to feature your titles in a library story hour, and any other creative ideas you may have. Some authors also offer printable pages for kids — coloring pages, puzzles, games and other activities.

Book Ordering Information

Of course, you want your site visitors to be able to purchase your books if they are interested in doing so!

- Bookstore/Publisher referrals — If your publisher allows direct orders, you can give them the publisher's toll-free number to call. Maybe you have a friendly relationship with a local bookstore that stocks your books, and you can give their number to site visitors. Some authors and illustrators choose to do this as a way to support independent children's bookstores.
- Online ordering — People are increasingly more comfortable ordering online, and enjoy the convenience of it. If your book is available online, it may encourage one of your site visitors to quickly turn into a customer. There are three ways to encourage online orders:

1. Provide a direct link to your favorite bookstore, your publisher (if they allow direct ordering online), or direct visitors to *www.abfc.com* (the Association of Booksellers for Children) or *www.booksense.com* (the American Booksellers Association's web program for independent booksellers).
2. Provide a link to one of the large online book retailers, like Amazon.com or Powell's Books. Both Amazon and Powell's offer an affiliate program, where a site's owner (in this case, you!) can earn a percentage back from every sale made to a customer visiting them via your site.
3. Add a shopping cart to your site, and sell your books yourself. Most authors and illustrators haven't chosen to do this, for several reasons. First of all, it's costly to set up and requires a special Internet "merchant account" enabling you to accept and approve credit cards. Second, it takes time to implement, meaning less time is available for writing and/or illustrating. Lastly, it puts the author in direct competition with bookstores (and in some cases, publishers), which can lead to uncomfortable conversations.

Writing Samples

Some authors include sample chapters or paragraphs taken from existing books, and others use "teaser" samples from forthcoming books as a promotional tool. If you keep adding new chapters of a new book, for example, it's an incentive for return visits to the site. This also gives site visitors a feeling of active involvement in an author's body of work.

Autographed Copies

Offering personally autographed copies of your books is another way to generate interest in your site, since you are offering something that isn't easily available anywhere else.

To make ordering convenient, you can include a fill-in order form on the site for visitors to print out and mail to you with a check. Remember to include space for them to tell you how they would like the book personalized, and also to include the shipping cost with your price information.

Art Portfolio

Scanning in and displaying samples of your art can be a fantastic way for illustrators to share their portfolio with editors, art directors and other potential clients.

Art for Sale

An illustrator's web site can be a showcase to promote art or book art products like greeting cards or posters. You should consider scanning in and displaying pictures of the art or products along with details about cost and how to order.

Marketing Your Web Site

Once you've created your own web site, it's important to actively promote it — to trade publications, associations, educators, librarians, parents and friends. Put your site address on your stationery, business cards, brochures and teacher guides. Ask your publisher to list it on promotional material about your books — jackets and biographies, for instance, and ask if they will link to your site from theirs. Set aside time each week to visit other sites and request that they link to your site. There are many good children's literature sites (some are noted in the Directory) with links to author/illustrator sites, so request that your site be added to their lists. When you do a school visit, be sure to encourage teachers and children to come and visit your site — before and after the visit. Submit your site name to search engines so that visitors can easily find it using Yahoo!, Google, or one of the other large search engines.

Email newsletter

An email newsletter is a useful way to keep visitors and potential customers informed about your work. It doesn't need to be lengthy and you don't want to send it too often. There are so many niche markets for children's books and email is a cost-effective method of reaching craft stores, garden stores, museum stores, zoos, historical societies and theme stores.

Updating Your Site

Keep in mind that, like a press kit, your site also needs constant updating. Check it often for errors, and periodically make revisions (update your travel schedule) or add new information (new links or a cover image of your forthcoming book). Adding new or updated content monthly is a good rule of thumb. You can easily and inexpensively refresh the look of your site with simple changes like a new color scheme, or adding a new title or featured book to your homepage. If it fits your personality, try adding sound clips of the music you listen to while writing or illustrating, or write something about the writers that have inspired you.

Viewing your site may be the first time someone is introduced to you and your work, and you want to make a good impression!

Should You Blog?

A blog, short for Weblog, is a Web site that contains brief entries arranged in reverse chronological order. Evan Williams, the creator of Blogger.com, describes them this way. "The blog concept is about three things: frequency, brevity and personality." Blogging software, is often free in a basic configuration. Popular free or low-cost services include blogger.com; typepad. com; wordpress.com and livejournal.com. An author blog can be used in conjunction with or instead of a Web site. Initial set up and online maintainance are easy, so your blog can feature current information on book-related activities. Blogs give readers a chance to develop a personal connection with you. One caveat, you have to make a commitment to update your blog frequently. Your readers will expect new blog entries to be posted daily or weekly updated.

Some Great Author Blogs

http://www.megcabot.com/blog/blogger.html
http://www.neilgaiman.com/journal/journal.asp
http://cynthialeitichsmith.blogsport.com/

Harness the Power of the Blogosphere

Whether or not you choose to join the blogosophere yourself, other bloggers can help you promote your books. Blogs published by teens, librarians, other authors, schools and public libraries review children's books.

Blogs written by Teaches, Writers and Librarians

These blogs are a great resource. Check with your publisher they may already be providing review copies to some of these prominent blogs.

http://yabookscentral.blogspot.com/
http://bookmoot.blogspot.com/

http://www.bookbuds.net
http://chickenspaghetti.typepad.com/chicken spaghetti/

Public Library Teen Web Sites and Blogs

Public Library children's and teen sites and blogs can be an effective medium for promoting your books. These blogs review books, announce events, list links to author blogs and sponsor online book clubs. They are a good place to publicize speaking engagements, school visits or book signings. If the Web site has a teen advisory board, the board members may be interested in reading advance copies of your book. The reach of these Web sites and blogs extends beyond the geographic area from which they originate. Teens from all over the country visit the larger library blogs.

Library Blogs

http://teenspace.cincinnatilibrary.org
http://kids.nypl.org/
http://www.teenspoint.org/

Web Sites and Blogs that Review Children's Books

Information about contacting the editors and where to send books can usually be found in the "contact us" section of a blog or Web site.

Sites with Reviews Written by Teens

Flamingnet
http://www.flamingnet.com/

Smart Girl
http://www.smartgirl.org/

Teenink
http://www.teenink.com/

Teenreads
http://www.teenreads.com/index.asp

Sites with Reviews Written by Adults

Children's Books at About.com
http://childrensbooks.about.com/

Favorite Teen Angst Books
http://www.grouchy.com/angst/index.html/

Genreflecting
http://www.genreflecting.com/Teen.html

Reading Rants
http://www.tin.lib.mi.us%7Eamutch/jen/index.html

The Cybils Awards

In 2006 a group of bloggers launched the Cyblic (Children's and YA Blogger's Library Awards.) The Cyblis operates on a new populist model in which anyone - young or old, expert or beginning reader - can nominate the books they love most. Awards are given for books in eight categories. A panel of bloggers conduct the first stage of judging. Then a second grou pf judges comprised of librarians, teachers, homeschoolers, authors and illustrators make the final decision in each category. For more information about the awards visit:

http://dadtalk.typepad.com/cyblis/2006/10/the cyblis judg.html

CHAPTER VIII

Taking The Next Step: Should You Hire An Agency?

Authors and illustrators often ask whether to hire an agency to do the kind of work described in this book. The purpose in writing this guide is to provide the tools needed to self-promote a children's book as you get established. This way, limited funds can be spent on marketing rather than service fees.

Once your career is well underway, and you know how you would like the marketing handled, based on your own expertise, you may find it more effective to hire an agency to supplement your work or take over the whole job. Keep in mind that an agency can be more effective with an author or illustrator who has a larger body of work to promote than it can be with one book, unless that book is particularly newsworthy. In selecting an agency, consider whether its style fits yours and whether it has particular expertise that relates to your books.

It can also be helpful to check with other authors and illustrators to find out what marketing they've done on their own or through an agency. Some have considered the idea of sharing resources and forming marketing groups, much the same way that authors use writing critique groups for peer support and input.

Keep in mind that marketing is a long-term process and that it takes time to find out what works best for you and your books.

CHAPTER IX

Directory

Information is current as of March 2007.

ASSOCIATIONS AND ORGANIZATIONS

American Association of Museums
1575 Eye Street, NW Suite #400
Washington, DC 20005
202-289-1818
www.aam-us.org
Mailing Lists:
Categorized by type of museum. Names are of museum directors. Call for price information.

American Booksellers Association, Inc.
200 White Plains Road
Tarrytown, NY 10591
914-591-2665
www.bookweb.org
Mailing Lists: General bookstore list.
Conventions: Spring convention and regional meetings throughout the year.
Publications: *Bookselling This Week*, available online
Membership: $350 per year

American Library Association
50 East Huron Street
Chicago, IL 60611
800-545-2433
www.ala.org

Awards: Newbery Medal for children's literature; Caldecott Medal for illustration; Printz Award for young adult literature; Sibert Medal for nonfiction; Coretta Scott King Awards for African-American authors and illustrators; Pura Belpré Medal for best book about the Latino experience; Schneider Family Book Awards for author or illustrator of a book about the disability experience; Odyssey Award for Excellence in Audiobook Production; and Theodor Seuss Geisel Award for author or illustrator of a book for beginning readers..

Conventions: Annual summer and mid-winter conventions. Regional meetings throughout the year.

Divisions: Association for Library Service to Children (ALSC)
www.ala.org/ala/alsc
Young Adult Library Services Association (YALSA)
www.ala.org/ala/yalsa
American Association of School Librarians (AASL)
www.ala.org/ala/aasl

Publications: ***Booklist***; ***Book Links***; ***Choice***; Annual notable children's book list published by ALSC; Recommended book lists published by YALSA.

Membership: Call for information.

Mailing lists are available; call for information

American Wholesale Booksellers Association
702 South Michigan
South Bend, IN 46601
574-288-4141
www.awba.com

Association Of Booksellers For Children
62 Wenham Street
Jamaica Plain, MA 02130
617-390-7759
www.abfc.com
Awards: E.B. White Read Aloud Award selected annually by members.
Conventions: Meet annually at the American Bookseller Association spring convention, Book Expo America.
Publications: quarterly newsletter.
Membership: $50 per year/Author/Illustrator
Contact: Kristen McLean, Executive Director
Mailing List: Available online.

Association for Childhood Education International
17904 Georgia Avenue, Suite 215
Olney, MD 20832
301-570-2111; 800-423-3563
www.acei.org
Conventions: Annual study conference, some regional meetings.
Publications: *Childhood Education* (reviews children's books). *Journal of Research in Childhood Education.*
Membership: $45 per year

Association of Children's Museums
1300 L Street N.W., Suite 975
Washington, DC 20005
202-898-1080
www.childrensmuseums.org
Publications: *Hand to Hand* (quarterly journal); *ACM News* (bi-monthly)

Membership: $250 per year
Member Directory: $50/members; $100/nonmembers

Association of Science Technology Centers
1025 Vermont Avenue, NW, Suite 500
Washington, DC 20005
202-783-7200
www.astc.org
Publications: *Dimensions* (news journal)
Mailing List: $200

Author's Guild
31 East 32nd Street, 7th Floor
New York, NY 10016
212-563-5904
www.authorsguild.org
Conventions: Annual meeting and panel discussions of interest to children's book authors throughout the year.
Publications: *Author's Guild Bulletin* (quarterly; general information for authors). They also do two mailings a year to their children's book authors on items of interest.
Membership: $90 per year

Catholic Library Association
c/o Sister Jean R. Bostley, SSJ
100 North Street, Suite 224
Pittsfield, MA 01201
413-443-2252
www.cathla.org
Awards: Regina Medal for a lifetime of excellence in writing books for children.
Conventions: Annual spring meeting and regional meetings throughout the year.

Publications: *Catholic Library World*
Membership: $45+ per year, individual

The Children's Book Council
12 West 37th Street, 2nd Floor
New York, NY 10018
212-966-1990
www.cbcbooks.org
Publications: Pamphlets, brochures, newsletter; Awards and Prizes Online, $150/year
Mailing List: $2.00, plus SASE
Membership: $60 one-time fee for lifetime subscription to semi-annual newsletter.

Library of children's books by member publishers open to public.

Christian Booksellers Association
PO Box 62000
Colorado Springs, CO 80962
719-265-9895, 800-252-1950
www.cbaonline.org
Conventions: Only open to retailers
Publications: *CBA Marketplace* (trade publication for the religious market).
Membership: $200

Educational Paperback Association
PO Box 1399
East Hampton, NY 11937
631-329-3315
www.edupaperback.org
Awards: Ludington Award presented annually
Conventions: Annual meeting open to members only

Top 100 Bestselling Author list updated annually, with links to author biographies.

International Reading Association

800 Barksdale Road
Newark, DE 19714
302-731-1600
www.reading.org

Awards: Children's Book Award for first or second work by an author; Lee Bennett Hopkins Promising Poet Award

Conventions: International spring convention and regional conventions throughout the year.

Publications: *The Reading Teacher* (pre-school/elementary), *Journal Of Adolescent And Adult Literacy*; *Lectura Y Vida* (Spanish, all levels); all include articles and reviews. *Reading Today* (member newspaper), *Reading Research Quarterly* (technical research journal).

Membership: $36 per year.

Jewish Book Council

520 8th Avenue, 4th Floor
New York, NY 10018
212-201-2920
www.jewishbookcouncil.org

Awards: Children's Book Award to the author of a children's book.

Publications: *Jewish Book World* (tri-annual publication with reviews of children's books); topical bibliographies of children's books.

Membership: Free.

Bookfair List: $50

Museum Store Association
4100 East Mississippi, Suite 800
Denver, CO 80246
303-504-9223
www.museumdistrict.com
Mailing Lists: List of museum store buyers, available by type of museum. Membership directory is free. Mailing labels (available to members) cost $150.
Membership: $145+

National Association for the Education of Young Children
1313 L Street, N.W., Suite 500
Washington, DC 20005
800-424-2460
www.naeyc.org
Conventions: Annual fall convention and affiliate conferences throughout the year.
Publications: *Young Children* (includes reviews of children's books); *Early Childhood Research Quarterly* (sponsor).
Membership: $35+ per year. Individual only.

National Catholic Education Association
1077 30th Street, NW, Suite 100
Washington, DC 20007
202-337-6232
www.ncea.org
Conventions: Annual spring convention and regional conventions throughout the year.
Publications: *Momentum* (quarterly magazine which includes reviews of children's books).
Membership: $150 individual

National Council of Teachers of English
1111 Kenyon Road, West
Urbana, IL 61801
877-369-6283
www.ncte.org
Awards: Award for Excellence in Poetry for Children given for a body of work; Orbis Pictus Award for outstanding nonfiction for children.
Publications: Book lists geared for different teaching levels.
Conventions: Annual conventions in the fall and spring and regional meetings throughout the year.
Membership: $40 per year

National Education Association
1201 16th Street, NW
Washington, DC 20036
202-833-4000
www.nea.org
Awards: Author-Illustrator Human and Civil Rights Award
Conventions: NEA Annual Meeting
Publications: *NEA Today*
Membership: Call for information

Parenting Publications of America
4929 Wilshire Boulevard, Suite 428
Los Angeles, CA 90010
323-937-5514
www.parentingpublications.org

PEN American Center
588 Broadway, Suite 303
New York, NY 10012
212-334-1660
www.pen.org

Conventions: Two group meetings per year.
Groups: Children's book authors committee
Publications: *PEN American Center Newsletter* (general interest), *PEN America Literary Journal.*
Membership: Call for details on membership requirements.

Publishers Marketing Association (PMA)
627 Aviation Way
Manhattan Beach, CA 90266
310-372-2732
www.pma-online.org
Awards: Benjamin Franklin Awards for the best books in various genres.
Membership: Call for information.

Society of Children's Book Writers and Illustrators
8271 Beverly Boulevard
Los Angeles, CA 90048
323-782-1495
www.scbwi.org
Awards: Golden Kite Awards for outstanding children's books in fiction and non-fiction. Magazine Merit Award for outstanding works of fiction, non-fiction, poetry, and illustration published in magazines for children. Awards are also given for best humor writing, new works, and art portfolio.
Grants: Provides work-in-progress grants for writers and illustrators who are members.
Conventions: Two national conventions, regional meetings and workshops throughout the year.
Publications: *Society of Children's Book Writers Bulletin* (newsletter). Pamphlets on a variety of subjects are available for the cost of postage.
Membership: $75 per year

CHILDREN'S AND TEEN BOOK CLUBS

Bookspan
501 Franklin Avenue
Garden City, NY 11530
516-490-4561
www.bookspan.com
Home book clubs for ages 6 mos.-12 yrs. Includes Children's Book of-the-Month Club and Kid's Book Planet

Scholastic Book Clubs
557 Broadway
New York, NY 10012
212-343-6100
www.scholastic.com
School book clubs for grades K-12. Includes Arrow, Firefly, TAB and TrollCarnival clubs.

INFORMATION SOURCES

American Book Trade Directory
Information Today, Inc.
143 Old Marlton Pike
Medford, NJ 08055
609-654-6266
www.infotoday.com
Lists book retailers and wholesalers throughout the United States and Canada.The directory also includes information on size, special subject areas, and regions covered.
Frequency: Updated annually.
Price: $299

American Library Directory
Information Today, Inc.
143 Old Marlton Pike
Medford, NJ 08055
609-654-6266
www.infotoday.com
Includes key information on public, academic and special libraries throughout the U.S. and Canada.
Frequency: Updated annually.
Price: $299 for two volumes

Bacon's Information, Inc.
332 South Michigan Avenue
Chicago, IL 60604
866-639-5087
www.bacons.com
Bacon's Newspapers/Magazine Directory (2 volumes, covers magazines & newspapers), 2007 edition, $450
Bacon's Radio, TV & Cable Directory (2 volumes), 2007 edition, $450
Bacon's Internet Media Directory (I volume, covers web sites), 2007 edition, $450
MediaCalendars.com; searchable editorial calendars, $200 per year
Online subscription to all directories except international, updated daily, $2,695

Chase's Calendar Of Events
McGraw Hill Companies
PO Box 548 (for individuals) -or-
PO Box 545 (for schools and businesses)
Blacklick, OH 43004
800-262-4729 (for individuals) -or-
800-323-4900 (for schools and businesses)
www.chases.com
Lists national holidays, regional and local events, special celebrations and observances throughout the year.
Frequency: Annual
Price: $64.95

Direct Marketing Association

1120 Avenue of the Americas
New York, NY 10036-6700
212-768-7277
www.the-dma.org
An organization that provides information on mailing list brokers and direct marketing consultants, and start-up information for new direct marketers.

Directory of Mail Order Catalogs

National Mail Order Association
2807 Polk Street, NE
Minneapolis, MN 55418
612-788-1673
www.nmoa.org
Frequency: Updated annually
Price: $250 (softcover)

D & B Direct Sales and Marketing Catalog

D & B Sales and Marketing Solutions
460 Totten Pond Road
Waltham, MA 02451
800-590-0065; 781-672-9200
www.zapdata.com
Directory of mailing lists available through Dun & Bradstreet. Catalog free upon request.

Encyclopedia of Associations

Thomson Gale
27500 Drake Road
Farmington Hills, MI 48331
800-877-4253
www.gale.com
Available in print and CD-ROM formats. Call for current price.

Gebbie Press All-In-One Directory
Gebbie Press
PO Box 1000
New Paltz, NY 12561
845-255-7560
www.gebbieinc.com
Single volume includes information on magazines, newspapers, radio and television networks and stations and syndicates in the United States.
Frequency: Updated annually.
Price: $165 for book. $565 for disk sets.

Literary Market Place
Information Today, Inc.
143 Old Marlton Pike
Medford, NJ 08055
800-300-9868
www.literarymarketplace.com
A comprehensive directory for the publishing industry that includes information on publishers, wholesalers, book clubs, production services, media and more.
Frequency: Updated annually.
Price: $299 for two volumes.

Market Data Retrieval
1 Forest Parkway
Shelton, CT 06484-1117
800-333-8802
www.schooldata.com
Offers mailing lists of the childcare, school and library market.

Quality Education Data, Inc. (QED)
1050 17th Street, Suite 1100
Denver, CO 80265
800-525-5811
www.qeddata.com
Offers mailing lists of the school and library market.

Radio-TV Interview Reports
Bradley Communications Corp.
135 East Plumstead Avenue
Landsdowne, PA 19050
610-259-0707
www.rtir.com
Magazine for talk show producers that accepts ads promoting books and authors.

INTERNET RESOURCES

Children's Authors Network
An authors' organization which provides meaningful school programs promoting literacy and the creative process.
http://www.childrensauthorsnetwork.com

Children's Literature Navigator
This is a compilation of Internet resources for librarians, parents, teachers, caregivers, and children.
http://childlitnavigator.imaginarylands.org

Children's Literature Web Guide
This well-known web site has a section called Authors and Illustrators on the Web.
www.ucalgary.ca/~dkbrown

Cooperative Children's Book Center (CCBC)
The CCBC is a unique examination, study and research library of the School of Education at the University of Wisconsin-Madison. The web site offers a wealth of information, including a section about authors and illustrators.
www.education.wise.edu/ccbc

The Purple Crayon
This site contains information about writing, illustrating and publishing children's books.
www.underdown.org

TeachingBooks.net
A mega-site providing easy, categorized access to information about authors, illustrators and book resources.
www.TeachingBooks.net

TRADE AND EDUCATION PUBLICATIONS

Book Links
50 East Huron Street
Chicago, IL 60611
800-545-2433
www.ala.org

Book Marketing Update
Open Horizons
P.O. Box 2887
Taos, NM 87571
505-751-3398
www.bookmarket.com

Booklist
50 East Huron Street
Chicago, IL 60611
800-545-2433
www.ala.org

Bookselling This Week
200 White Plains Road
Tarrytown, NY 10591
914-591-2665
www.bookweb.org

Bulletin of the Center for Children's Books
501 East Daniel Street
Champaign, IL 61820
217-244-0324
www.lis.uiuc.edu/puboff/bccb

CBA Marketplace
9240 Explorer Drive
Colorado Springs, CO 80920
800-252-1950
www.cbaonline.org

Catholic Library World
100 North Street, Suite 224
Pittsfield, MA 01201-5109
413-443-2252
www.cathla.org

Horn Book Magazine and Horn Book Guide
56 Roland Street, Suite 200
Boston, MA 02129
800-325-1170; 617-628-0225
www.hbook.com

Independent Publisher
Jenkins Group
400 West Front Street, S. 4A
Traverse City, MI 49684
231-933-0445
www.independentpublisher.com

Instructor
557 Broadway, 3rd Floor
New York, NY 10012
212-343-6110; 800-724-6527
www.scholastic.com/Instructor

Kirkus Reviews
770 Broadway/ 6th Floor
New York, NY 10003
646-654-4602
www.kirkusreviews.com

Learning
P.O. Box 9753
Greensboro, NC 27429
877-696-0825
www.learningmagazine.com

Publishers Weekly
360 Park Avenue South
New York, NY 10010
646-746-6758
www.publishersweekly.com

School Library Journal
SLJ also publishes a supplement, Curriculum Connections
360 Park Avenue South
New York, NY 10010
646-746-6759
www.slj.com

Teacher
6935 Arlington Road, Suite 100
Bethesda, MD 20814
800-346-1834
www.teachermagazine.org

Teaching K-8
40 Richards Avenue
Norwalk, CT 06854
800-249-9363
www.teachingK-8.com

VOYA (Voice of Youth Advocates)
4501 Forbes Blvd., Suite 200
Lanham, MD 20706
888-486-9297
www.voya.com

WHOLESALERS AND BOOK CHAINS

This section lists only companies mentioned elsewhere in this book. Other wholesalers are found in *Literary Market Place* or by contacting the American Wholesale Booksellers Association. Booksellers can be located through the American Booksellers Association.

WHOLESALERS

Baker & Taylor, Inc.
2550 West Tyvola Road,
Suite 300
Charlotte, NC 28217
800-775-1800
www.btol..com

Bookazine Co., Inc.
75 Hook Road
Bayonne, NJ 07002
201-339-7777
www.bookazine.com

Book Wholesalers, Inc. (BWI)
1847 Mercer Road
Lexington, KY 40511
800-888-4478
www.bwibooks.com

The Booksource
1230 Macklind Avenue
St. Louis, MO 63110
800-444-0435
www.booksource.com

Brodart Company
Books Division
500 Arch Street
Williamsport, PA 17701
800-233-8467
www.brodart.com

Follett Library Resources
1340 Ridgeview Drive
McHenry, IL 60050
815-759-1700; 888-511-5114
www.flr.follett.com

Ingram Book Company
1 Ingram Boulevard
P.O. Box 3006
La Vergne, TN 37086-1986
800-937-8000
www.ingrambook.com

Partners Book Distributing Inc.
2325 Jarco Drive
Holt, MI 48842
517-694-3205

Perma-Bound Books
617 E. Vandalia Road
Jacksonville, IL 62650
Phone: 800-637-6581 or 217-243-5451
www.perma-bound.com

Sagebrush Education Resources
Corporate Office
1391 Corporate Drive
McHenry, IL 60051
800-533-5430
www.sagebrushcorp.com

CHAINS AND INTERNET BOOKSELLERS

Amazon.com
1200 12th Avenue South
Seattle, WA 98144
206-622-2335
www.amazon.com

Barnes & Noble
122 5th Avenue
New York, NY 10011
212-633-3300
www.barnesandnoble.com

Books-A-Million
402 Industrial Lane
Birmingham, AL 35211
205-942-3737; 800-201-3550
www.booksamillion.com

Borders
100 Phoenix Drive
Ann Arbor, MI 48108
734-477-1100
www.borders.com

INDEX

A

B

C

D

E

F

G

H

I

J

K

L

M

N

P

Q

R

S

T

V

W

Y

NOTES

NOTES